I0234252

Grooming Milo

Written by **Marina Hood**

Illustrated by **Nadia Ronquillo**

LiveLifeHappy Publishing

LiveLifeHappy
Publishing

Copyright © 2024 by Marina Hood.

All rights reserved.

Published and Distributed in The United States of America by Live Life Happy Publishing.
livelifehappypublishing.com

All rights reserved. No part of this book may be reproduced by any mechanical, photographic, or electronic process or in the form of a phonograph recording, Nor may it be stored in a retrieval system, transmitted, or otherwise be copied for public or private use- other than for "fair use" as brief quotations embodied in articles and reviews without prior written permission of the author. If you use any of the information in this book for yourself, which is your constitutional right, the author and the publisher assume no responsibility for your actions.

Library of Congress Cataloging-in-Publication Data
Hood, Marina
Grooming Milo
Author: Marina Hood
marinahood.com
Illustrator: Nadia Ronquillo
nadiaronquilloart.com
Juvenile Fiction - Humorous - Pets & Animal Care
Children's Picture Books - Animals - Humorous
Family Life - Humorous - Dogs
ISBN Paperback Book ISBN 978-1-990461-68-2

Live Life Happy Publishing
Publisher's Note & Author DISCLAIMER
This publication is designed to provide accurate and authoritative information concerning the subject matter covered. It is sold with the understanding that the publisher and author are not engaging in or rendering any psychological, medical or other professional services.
The contents of this book are the opinions and perspectives of the author alone and not necessarily those of the publishing house.

To my beloved Milo.
Your memory will forever reside in our hearts.
Rest in peace, sweet Milo.

Milo needs a haircut.

MILO

"Let's go, Nicole!"
said Mom.
"It's time to take Milo
to the dog groomer."

Mom said Milo needs to get groomed by an expert.
Grooming Milo must be hard work.

DOG GROOMING

Grooming Services Include:
Basic Groom
Full Groom
Basic Wash
Nail Trim
Ears Cleaned
Teeth Brushing

OPEN

HOURS	
MON	CLOSED
TUE	8am - 6pm
WED	8am - 6pm
THU	8am - 6pm
FRI	8am - 6pm
SAT	9am - 5pm
SUN	9am - 5pm

I can't wait to see Milo groomed!

"Welcome!" said the groomer.

"Hello, this is our poodle Milo," replied Mom.
"We have a grooming appointment."

DOG GROOM

PET

DOGGY

CAT
NIP

"What a sweet puppy!" said the groomer.
"Are we doing a Poodle Cut today?"

"No, thank you," replied Mom.
"Shaved hair and pompoms are not for Milo."

DOG GROOM

"Milo just needs a simple haircut, nothing too fancy,"
said Mom.

"Okay, I'll call you when he's ready,"
said the groomer.

DOG GROOM

KIT
MISS
ROYA
DOG CHO
PRO D

MILO

10

Four hours later...

HOURS
MON CLOS
TUE 8am -
WED 8am -
THU 8am -
FRI 8am -
SAT 9am -
SUN 9am -

"Welcome back!"
said the groomer.
"Milo is ready for you."

Mom thought Milo's haircut was a little too fancy, but I loved it!

KITTY CAT

MISSY

ROYAL DOG

DOG GROOM

DOG

PET

DOGGY

CATTY

CAT NIP

Dad was also surprised to see Milo's fancy haircut.

"I'm sure the groomer will get it right next time," added Mom.

"I don't think we need the groomer anymore," said Dad.

"Let's groom Milo ourselves. It can't be that difficult!"

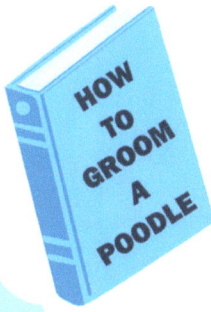

15

Two months later...

"I'm ready to give
Milo a nice haircut!"
said Dad.

Mom tried to talk Dad out of grooming Milo.

"Don't worry, honey," said Dad.

"Milo is going to look great!"

17

That weekend...

Dad said he needed
a helper.

PET STORE

We gave Milo a warm bath.

We got him nice and dry.

We clipped his nails and
cleaned his ears.

19

Dad took out the new hair clippers and began cutting Milo's hair.

Dad must be an expert because he was cutting very fast.

We were almost done when Mom came outside.

"Oh no!" exclaimed Mom.

"What happened to Milo?"

The next morning...

Mom scheduled an appointment with the groomer.

Dad, Milo, and I went to the pet store to return the grooming supplies.

Mom felt a little embarrassed when going on walks with Milo.

I still had fun with Milo, even if he looked funny!

Two months later...

"Let's go, Nicole!" said Mom.
"It's time to take Milo to the dog groomer."

CALENDAR

NOVEMBER

Monday	Tuesday	Wednesday	Thursday	Friday	Saturday	Sunday
	1	2	3	4	5	6
7	8	9	10	11	12	13
14	15	16	17	18	19	20
21	22	23	24	25	26	27
28						

"Milo is ready for a Poodle Cut now,"
said Mom.

Four hours later...

The End

Milo almost 3 months old and ready for a haircut

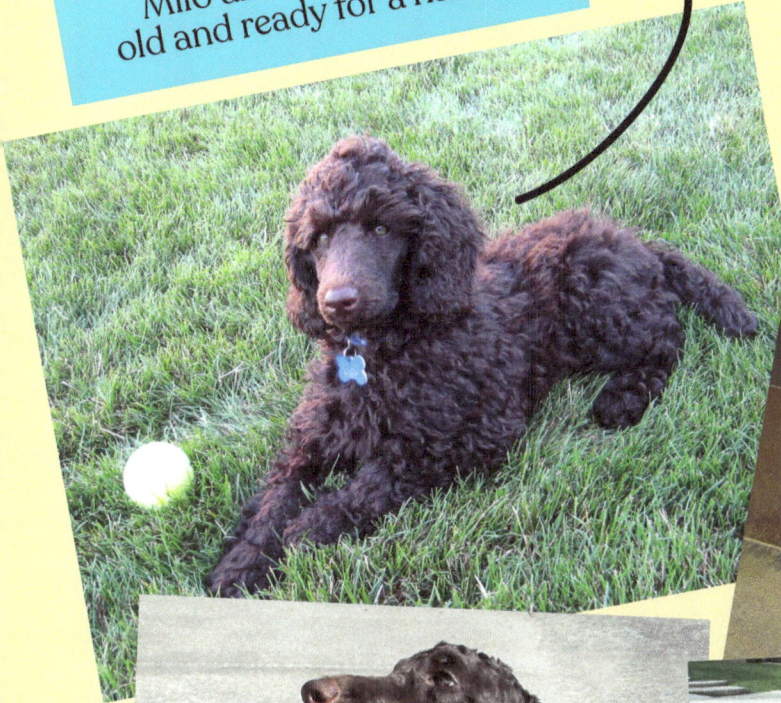

Milo after getting his first professional haircut

Milo after getting groomed by Dad

Milo after getting a professional Poodle Cut

About the Author

Marina Hood is a life & leadership coach, a mindfulness meditation teacher, and a children's book author. Her family has roots in both Colombia and Mexico. Marina has been a member of the Society of Children's Book Writers and Illustrators since 2009. She hopes to bring endless joy to children of all ages through her stories. Marina lives in San Diego, California. For more information, you can visit her website at marinahood.com

About Milo

Milo (June 17, 2008 - July 18, 2023) was a high-energy and affectionate chocolate brown poodle. He was a cherished member of Marina's family for over 15 years, bringing boundless love and joy into their lives. Throughout the years, Milo was the source of countless amusing and unforgettable moments, inspiring Marina to compile them into a delightful collection of stories.

About the Illustrator

Nadia Ronquillo is a children's book illustrator, a visual development artist, and a content creator from Ecuador. Her work can be found in children's books, animated shorts and television, with inspiration drawn from animated films. Nadia is an active innovator, contributing to projects and winning awards in Latin America and Europe, and her clients include major publishing companies. Nadia lives in coastal Guayaquil, the largest city in Ecuador. Living in such a warm and charming city influences her warm and bright color palettes. You can visit her at nadiaronquilloart.com

www.ingramcontent.com/pod-product-compliance
Lightning Source LLC
LaVergne TN
LVHW072059070426
835508LV00002B/169